D1614417

¡Pupitre, sí, toda la vida; púlpito
también, toda la muerte!

Cesar Vallejo

LIFE IS A PLATFORM

PETER LEVI
Life is a Platform

Anvil Press Poetry
associated with Routledge & Kegan Paul

B. 1.

First published in 1971
by Anvil Press Poetry
69 King George Street London SE10
Distributed by Routledge & Kegan Paul Ltd
Cloth SBN 900977-66-3
Paper SBN 900977-67-1
Fifty numbered copies of this edition
printed on Abbey Mills antique laid paper
have been signed by the author
SBN 900977-68-X
© Peter Levi 1971
Printed in England by The Lavenham Press Ltd

Acknowledgments
Some of these poems have previously appeared
in *Agenda, Carcanet* and *New Measure*

for Miranda and Iain

OMENS IN THE pear trees and in the mist.
Continual winters sicken the mind
with voice after voice of wind after wind,
hammers as cold and black as they can be.
Blue and gold the cold air of tomorrow
waits for the mason's gang and line of sky
that will dangle rough fruit in the green tree.

When the Rope Broke

THERE WAS THIS rope-end trailing over him.
It whipped and snapped. The light scalded his eyes.
The mountain swung around him in the air
and rock by rock broke outwards from his hand.
At dusk they found him pale and loosely lying
grasping and grasping in his silent mind
at five enormous thistles, two stonechats
and between eddies of the mountain mist
deep-feathered hawks on burning bracken wing,
slate-coloured water mountain darkening.

Didactic Poem

for Iain Watson

LINGERING TIME itself records itself, —
think time is over, say good-bye to it;
bird after bird expires into belief,
the sun among the stationary trees
touches the blue to level green and white:
there are no riddles in remarks like these.

Some of the young are poets I suppose
picking about in one another's lines
cobwebbing their own eyesight in shadows:
austere nature has ways to execute
the lively figures of her rough designs,
time is their voice and nature strikes them mute.

Time moves among the frosty rushes where
the daylight dies out with a rasping sound, —
these are the shortest days of the whole year,
trailing from fog to fog through seas of dew;
the ruffled birds desert the startled ground,
streams run in chains of ice, and weeds grow few.

Think time is over, say good-bye to it,
taking new words to make a new season;
draw bleak horizons working by lamp-light,
and let your eyes rest with a new surprise
on men and steel and jobs they use it on
and on the wild birds settling in their eyes.

13

MACHIAVELLI's evil role
was loving the state more than his soul;
having no soul to give away
would be the best role in the play.

14

A DOG BARKED in the night. Somewhere a lamp
shone through mist or a train was passing.
All that air, all that darkness
fuming with weeds and the quiet canals.
And what is it that aches and endures?
A train breaks open the black distances,
cold air, the taint of cinders and of leaves
infects my tongue. Awake before morning.
Not a mouse. Not a bird.
Last night two violins on the wireless
like rivers too cold for the swan to breed.
Rivers in Poland and in Germany
have left smells on my body and my hair.
You ask, Will there be peace before Christmas?
We travel on. The garden
is unable to speak, able to speak.

15

THE LONG TRAIN swings. In carriages alone
we dip cold faces in sweet-smelling prose
are ignorant of the world I suppose,
the journey wears us inward to the bone.

Honey and darkness and a private thought.
Saffron to blue. The New Year come and gone.
Each morning sky shipwrecks the Parthenon.
Girls in the trees Apollo never caught.

Feed on some molten drippings of the sun,
wheel in the wind, the glittering dark blue
of the wild sea, canaries singing true
all day in prison in deserts of stone.

The sea marries its island in the end:
the waterfront shakes out in a long line
saying one name, there are glasses of fine
basil and a few roses have ripened.

Paint up your crumbling house, live there alone,
cape and rock magnify in the dry light,
the ragged sea breaks to a dazzling white;
thrushes twitter in the whale's skeleton.

For John Caute (1965)

IF YOU or I could see
the south of Italy
when it .was pure forest
and uneroded rocks
were green and silver clocks,
a shallow grassy breast,

when there was no rock chapel,
when the delicious apple
of technics was unbitten,
suppose there was no doubt,
nothing to write about,
and nothing had been written:

should we have crossed the stream
from the nightmare or dream,
kicking up spray around us?
Sleep-people who are all
human, all animal,
would I suppose have found us.

Should we have built tree-huts
among the sweet chestnuts
or dug deep hiding-places?
Need it have ever ceased,
the beast-god and god-beast,
stub horns, enquiring faces?

Urbanity the note,
the sea-foam-purple throat
pulling the heroes in?
Could I have done much better
than this poem and letter
and map to travel in?

The dead world in the trees
has drier mysteries
than the dry year's death-rattle;
trees among trees in leaf
look like a dead belief
after an autumn battle.

Do you and I suppose
white rock with blue shadows,
the cold ash of the ages,
and stunted second growth,
broken up land, uncouth
caverns and hermitages

are really what arouses
mosquitoes and mean houses,
mad dogs, abandoned metal?
The truth is what we see;
what grows is Italy:
the dust will never settle.

Further away the Greek
mountains from peak to peak
climb their amazing lines,
and if they wreck the sun
the blood of air will run
bluer than when it shines.

Only we get the grace
to write in such a place
who can never forgive:
and learning how to hate
write chiefly for a time
when the sweet wish to live
will have died out in it.

ALL THAT WEIGHT of stone and of brick
rearing and toppling in my father's dreams
and the black-shadowed ruins in his times
have buried my life though I am awake,

now after years the landslide is moving
I have learned how to hope delicately
for some light fur of grass and a fruit tree
to fear no one to be sure of nothing.

I say the sea is in: the new spirit
is bluer than knowledge or industry,
weed-green for life, art will be swept away,
in our lives Europe is saying goodnight.

Despair is not in the intellect,
it is experience not a belief,
bitterness is a kind of forgiving,
and I am freedom's lover and addict.

19

THE BREAK OF DAY and the falling of night
birds fish moths in their generations
come without date: there is no infinite:
sea, rock and fossil are my creations.

Poetry without time is a sun-flame
flickering on the misty sea-surface
conversation has always been the same,
seen naked its body has strength and grace:

and I consider I have no future
but sea-blasted roses and foreshore grass,
the strongest languages are most impure,
I wear love on my chest like a horse-brass.

O unwritten poem, secret mountain
peaks, bogmyrtle, bracken and idle men,
handfuls of birds in handfuls of rain,
repeat these words once and forget them then.

SMOKE WHEN THE SUN fell and when it rose,
girls in their fresh white stinking of jasmine
women on mules their mouths smelling of wine;
the children played on dusty pianos.

Winter, you can remember backwards to
cigars and dying apples in the mist;
tunes and bad weather like a hand at whist,
I shift barley too dusty to see through.

Dreaming you can no longer understand
these times although they fall like a footfall,
now to wake is a kind of refusal,
anemones wake stone-cold in your hand.

The confused breasts of so many mountains,
too much rock, who can understand it?
One gulf is silver the sun fingers it
like a boy with a whistle while it rains.

No clock strikes with a perfectly clear chime,
dogs and lorry engines wake up together.
Dying women can prophesy the weather.
But I shall not be awake at that time.

St Valentine's Day

HUNGRY DOVES in a parliament of birds
shiver with love: their white communities
express a kind of gurgled discontent
through pouted breast, wild eyes and wheezy song:
and all thrushes call imprudently loud
breaking a hush from hillside to hillside,
that kind of music is no argument.
But the blinded, imprisoned nightingale,
the small canary and the quayside greenfinch
will infinitely vary one complaint
until dead shadows hang like draperies
over the heads of the birds' parliament.
Yet I know that the strongest and angriest
bird is the lover swan in his movement.

SNOWY WARS, snow-muffled fruit trees,
a clear moment, a long, bellowing train:
this coughing on the platform, this cognac,
the reeds and floods, the city in the rain,
the prison wall, you can never go back.

Say what it was, what were you looking for
in the darkness, in the trees, in the cold?
My brother who has for so long understood
the fruit on the fruit trees and is lost now.
Reading all night you get cold, you get cold.
The Rome express goes screaming through the wood.

They burnt it down in nineteen forty one.
Why is the wind dry and the dawn dry?
Darkness is in my mind; it is his time;
a musty smell where the birds have nested,
green bushes where the birds will not reply.
The station lamps light you enough really.
Roses have eaten them. This was my crime.

For Joan and Paddy

FIFTY YEARS AGO I might have died.
Nothing is growing in the villages
but scraggy wheat: *ploutos* repurified.
The children are in leaf darker than trees.
I think there are bare voices in the stars.
The mutterings of those cold fires are wars.

Something died and has come alive in us,
it withers cobble stones and old railings;
beautiful poverty was victorious,
I am fighting the coherence of things.
All my true-seeming words will shake to pieces
when my lamp dies and the dawn cold increases.

Labouring all night on the moon's dark side
I built an iron train: that train is full;
but might have died where Agamemnon died
slowly threshing the water like a gull,
and am in love with cuttings in the rock
where the muse cuckoos like a cuckoo clock.

I have built nothing in thirty-five years
except five wooden gates into a wood.
I sweated mist, beach pebbles were my tears,
red and white dawns which I have understood
broke into cold, and dried up in the end.
The people have no flag left to defend.

There is nothing in providence but leaves,
there is nothing in my heaven but stone;
no one in mountain villages believes
what I believe when I am alone;
the hammer strikes again and again,
it is the gold and silver age again.

Men are like birds and have their building times,
a man's wing will be free and his cheek red,
birds in his hand, not anything that rhymes,
sparkshowers shadows metal compacted,
a note so true that not one bird can sound it,
but whole ages of years stand still around it.

For Miranda

PEBBLES, ASHES, swill of the black water,
the rain flashed lightning, smelt of kitchen herbs,
it thundered on that night, you were awake
banging the iron blanket, one free hand
like fire burning without wires in the air,
the sea, the wind, the whistle and the roar.

Washed up. The waves are slamming their green doors.
And the wrecked sea still riding in the sky
crowded with lilac till late afternoon,
we were tied to the yellow riding light:
foundered: your eye the darkest it has been
and your breath rougher than the surf's cold breath.

Stepping out say like trees through blue daylight
my groin tangled in leaves I am freedom;
generations of red and white water birds,
that strong dark green, how quickly a fish dies,
pitching across the jetty like a deck,
the whitest lightning I have ever seen.

Season there can be no resurrection.
Do not die, do not believe in death,
good God, you are as pure as a sea-pebble,
sinking into sea-ashes in the sea.
I tell you in that storm nothing can live
but what is without life, and true, and free.

For Miranda and Iain

DROWSY TREE. In the end it revives
and the sky suddenly begins to flash
scattering masses of the mist and leaves;
abundant pure smells, then the thundercrash:
Apollo barks, the god's in his machine,
the light is mine and the darkness is mine.

The last calamity is love of life,
it is my only tears, the ghost of God
wears away nature, live by this belief,
it wears us down, the darkness is wasted,
night birds like shreds of dawn are repeating
nothing, the cold the light sweats is nothing.

Look now. The buckling wheels of the sun's car
drop shadows of metal on the dead men:
there are wild birds whose voices express fear
who will not abandon my body then;
it is the kindly work of the rock-dove
to drop pure water in the mouth of love.

The moral dark of poems is over,
they set to impenetrable crystal:
batlight, the moon's detritus running clear,
the stars' burnt feathers hissing as they fall;
listen: it is the Word with scything wings
purging the sky of his imaginings.

God is soughing in the country silence.
It is common to love one another.

When the sun rises it troubles my sense.
That smoky redness is God in his fire.
There was no one else: therefore the prophet.
Speaking in words the rock-face will forget.

28

AND A LOST SUMMER at a dying point
woods enough hills enough and words enough:
weeds, the dank humus and one eye of light.
Trees and words look loosely. They were not meant.
What is not loose and cannot speak is love.

Out in the miles long looking fields of grain
one tanned roebuck as dark as a raincloud
running like death, freedom is untrodden,
the ragged trees are a dark battle-line
gunning the tattered air over the road.

There is still something in the exhausted soil
clean of association, will break clear,
like a late river cloudier than steel
where avenues of leaves coil and uncoil,
like night grass, and fireworms as cold as fear.

What is not loose and cannot speak is love.
Not what she is but she is what they are.
I will be the mad hermit of these woods,
life is a coarse language, it shall be love,
I say nothing shall speak but what they are.

29

THIS FIRE that walked ankle-deep in the sea
confusing stones and fringes of the sea
was God's fire. There are seasons in your mind.
So few stones. Nothing I understand.
Always like this, dumbfounded by the sea.

You drop shadows on my page of long lines.
There is no rest in God and his designs.
My poetry is the dumbness of life:
buds of darkness, tree-blossoms of belief,
and the cloud-bird, his long and longer lines.

Crying inward through rainy atmospheres:
there is not so strange music in the spheres.
I am silence, and these voices will die.
There is pure fire in God and in his eye;
the sea revives through fiery atmospheres.

Your mind is words ripped off from air and light,
night smells of branches in the sea and light:
there is no fire in my understanding:
dark leaf of life: there is no forgiving
the coldness of breath when it becomes light.

30

THEN ONE DAY by the window in the new place,
to sniff the tree-line, hear an obscure thrush,
lifts open something inside the whole sky,
this ruffle-feathered bird in a rank bush
proclaims I love, I do not love, and why.

No one understands these beginnings,
the beginning of daylight, the apple-blush
declines yellow, the rough and heavy sea
dies and is revelation and the thrush
will say I cannot love, love is in me.

White drops of fire hang crazy overhead:
what time has begun, what life will finish.
The raving of the bird in the dawn-flush
was language and it is a dying wish:
it is the new ruins, the desert grass.

IT HAPPENED. A head bleeding on a high pole.
The sea quietly makes in, appears to lap
sweet liquors, green spheres on the table-cloth,
like the low hum of an important conversation.
Little swell, a provincial reputation.
The waves slam like trump after trump.
The patent shoe, the plastic cuff, the army
in leather and in linen. Heavy steel.
Waves pouring over that machinery.
There will be salt in the sky on that morning.

Song

O simple love
this happy man
will not lie down
and be alone
until in death
he must lie down
O simple life

NOTHING HAS BEEN written about this life.
I am a glacier, I am a rose
as blonde as honey smells of narcissus,
cattle-eyed, the skin dusty but not rough;
white trees are mysteries, the wood is life.

I can tell you this whole wood is bare trees:
what you can smell is the greenness of must
and a white solid blanket of ground-mist,
heavy sleep is the best I can advise
then become wooden-breasted like the trees.

This bible hermit has his kind of life:
his reward is to live thirty years wild
crouching in grass like a hare in a field;
trickles of rain give him water enough,
the truth of his bible is in his life.

34

THE SKY CLEARED and we came to an island
fresher than daisies greener than sunshine
the mountain spouted fire, it was God's land.

We saw a virgin standing in the cave
greener than daisies fresher than sunshine
her shadows and that fruit are all we have.
The storm has not cleared. We are in the storm.

One day was clear, the evening gilt and green,
shooting long shadows, it could mean no harm,
the sea will be where the island has been.
It is dark now. We use life in the storm.

35

WHEN DOES IT END? When does a new poem
ever end? It ends with the island.

Boats, where green watered Puritanic sand
carries offshore beyond the twelve mile limit
yelp and squall of the wind, musk of the girls,
the sailor knew his sweetheart in that wind.

We move through sleep, silently and alone.
Then rises to the surface glowering
it is a tree growing
a lyric poem will have no deadline.

The wrapped roses smelling of paper
are pure explosions of reason
and have no end to them. Modern times;
we are some kind of lover in the end.

I love those most who have no role in life.
        Nothing awake.

Poetry is reason, a slow coming awake.
The world was waiting for lyric poems.
Reasons conjoined, work of the body,
and language cannot be sweetened
but freedom is the burning cigarette
on everyone's lips.
The word of reason when it is awake.

Time's harvest is not in the loose life of my dreams
island beyond island beyond island

when I am awake.

Silence

THE BOMBS are finished.
It is silent.
We live hanging two or three hours in midair
in seats of steel like birdmen in childhood.
They disappeared into the cold.
Flamed in the misty nostrils of the sun.
How many villages?
I am holding on my hat.
Can you say what these people will do now?

The Captain scribbled, covering his hand,
Maybe I am the silence.

This paper is thirty prison islands.

Freedom torn into pieces in my hat.
Look. I shall empty this hat in the hedge.
Purer than water and stronger than grass.

37

TREE OF ROSES. The water crashed headlong
tearing the darkness out of the stone face.
A god of war might be a god of song.
The sign of faith is a physical grace:
thinness colour and smell like Asian clover,
the informal appearance of a lover.
Water is religion, it has no voice,
but drowns the silence of God in its noise.
There is no life to be had in the pure air,
and passion for goodness not having it
is rank swan-music and water-spirit.
Ice and a hundred moving points of fire:
the monks in the illuminated cave
only love what cannot love and will save.

In England morning colours like fruit-skin,
it darkens again with a whisp of light:
apple-trees to work at, grass to play in,
the blossom in the deepest woods is white.
That sun is cultivated, the sky even:
the god of song can love nothing but heaven.
He is exploding stars, the piston-rod
in the sky's dying engine, true and good.
His sudden, light drumming in a back street:
what passes is love, it is not belief,
love's religion is destructive of life
it is the heavy seed in the pale wheat.
Death shakes out the last words, what they release
is the old god of nature and of peace.

Living in the religion of peace
where God is outward, the world ingrowing,
I break my life to pieces in my voice,

to be like God in his imagining:
the origin of goodness was a fable
piety cast off made it available:
passion for goodness is love in the end,
it is broken language nothing can mend.
The throaty agitation of the trees,
snowinfected, colourstained by the air,
expresses green nature like a despair:
whatever lives has inward boundaries.
God has none, he is natured like a stone
frosteaten and sunbitten and alone.

39

Riddle

WITHOUT ME there is no person.
You would die by what I live on.
Thistles can be a skeleton.
The element of rock is height,
the broken rocks I cannot eat are my delight.

My limbs are chaos in motion,
the dusty coat, the dead lion,
my breath was sugar, it is gone.
The element is dry and bright,
the broken rocks I cannot eat are my delight.

The blue immense murdered my swan
my yellow and my green and brown.
Blind I am cold, my eye is sun,
I have voices that live on light,
the broken rocks I cannot eat are my delight.

WOOROO OF WILD birds in a ragged garden.
A gunshot hardly motions them at all
banging away at sixpence in the wall.
I choose peace, and the dumbness of this season.

The pink weeds in midriver on the island
and the thin poplar woods are without weight,
air scored with branches, branches scored with light,
walnut and willow give the sun day-shadow.

It has a house maybe of a rough texture,
hollyhocks and great sarsens of granite
(splashed ochre and a kind of silver-white)
decorate the rough hills time hardly grazes.

Things pile up an analogous confusion;
these old sunflowers hallooing the sun
extend themselves as if death were someone,
or snowy quiet not the one dimension.

41

BUSHROSES HANGING crumpled a leaf drops,
time is new extent minute by minute,
lives easily in wet, dark middle air,
green fruit will hang stains of colour on it.

Age-ease is no profound intuition,
it is dark extent, future memory,
can move freely in the horizon of one hour:
spirit is breath, lighter than time can be.

Buddha is in nature, in my nature,
and silver and solid as a time-piece:
the richness in the Victorian dark;
the sun's whisper troubles Buddha's increase.

Full snow-rivers tear away the whole track,
rock-dust withers and it is sediment.
Poplar and willow make light architecture,
and green embroidery on the blue tent.

THE STAIN IS in my liver and my brains
and my strength is a carcase of soupbones.
Heaven is swirling like a summer cloud,
there is no salt in the weak taste of blood,
the spirit blows to tatters in thin trees
and whines and cannot reach the provinces.
The angry mewing of the party chief
sours the bloodbath by indicating if.
He will become paper, become God,
a paper taste alternative to blood.

43

AGAINST THIS there is no poem then.
Big mountainsides where the small sheep are creeping,
mosswater weeping,
will see the end of Christ and his brethren.

The last trumpet: it is guerrilla war,
the one-eyed helicopters have gone hunting,
the deer are drunken
and I am drunk on the light breath of this star.

God changes what humans are conscious of,
we are old children, glass is our essence,
we give acceptance,
we know prisons, we are conscious of love.

44

GROWING MINT is a pleasure of penance.
When I was twentyfive I was in France,
I saw nothing naked and virginal,
nor did I play tennis, nor ever shall.

Flowerpots of red and white double stock
are political issues, I am still on the hook.
Watering cans and string are a mystery
to me, but this is the honey in history.

I am wagging my tongue like an animal,
in theatres there is no music at all,
in the past world lilac was ordinary,
may mornings, what you could smell, what you could see.

Sigh and roar! Night is your continent,
grass under moon, the simple and decent,
where what is virginal in the coming world
feeds in the dark; it is still crisp and cold.

45

SUMMER IS WINTER, spring will be autumn.
The fruit of the peartree and appletree
make the brown hooknosed eagle roll his eyes
to meet the mild eyes of the English dove.

46

Ballad

UNDER THE HOLLOW hooves of the rough-coated ponies
a lost valley muttering to an audience of mountains,
stranded in a wild country in the mouth of midnight
Phyllis was running, running after Corydon.

Loosely behind the light hooves of the night-coated horses
thunder sighed in the heather to an audience of mountains,
through a perpetual autumn of rocks rivers were raving,
Phyllis went crying, calling after Corydon.

Under the liquid hooves of the advancing, circling riders
one bird screamed in the grass to an audience of mountains,
lost in the shivering daylight, tired of the barren starlight
Phyllis ran screaming, screaming after Corydon.

Louder than the crashing hooves of the enormous riders
the sky cracked, birds were silent, rain tumbled in torrents,
in the vast grottoes of loneliness and the green caves of sorrow
Phyllis went weeping, weeping to an audience of mountains.

Quiet. The light, beautiful thunder of the receding horses;
Corydon stirred in his death like the flowering plants in the ocean.
In a never-ending country where all the trees are uneasy,
white and cold and dead under an audience of mountains.

47

THIS SPASM when I write and the disorder of my dreams,
this *tremor cordis* in the newspapers, wordy extremes,
all these bell-tones and noises chime the age away,
and God will make them come true in the street one day.
There is heaven in the destruction of this star,
and some philosophy where peace and pleasure are.
I say in the kingdom of the blind music is king
but liberty, reason and life have the most meaning.
Eighteen forty eight and nineteen fourteen
have blotted out democracy as if it had never been.
I say we shall see that generation again.
And God shall fulfil this with his amen.

48

Greek Folksong

ON AN APPLE, sweet apple, heavy apple tree
a hawk was searching in the branches of an appletree.

'I want to build a nest in your branches, apple tree.'
'Fine feathered hawk, such a thing cannot be,
you are scattering my blossom and the fruit drops out of me.'

49

Notebook / Homage to Brancusi

NEW GROVES of rough blue heads. Thin. Wild. The sun
    has not been absent.
Nor the rain in ruffled feathers.

In clouded farms, on cobbled yards, among the loose dung
    and the warm straw smelling of horse-piss, walks
    one white pigeon.
for poetry to be quiet
your hair is rougher than wool

O my unwritten poem, old and white biplane
nature was self-consumed and unforeseen: I beach
    my boat and paint it up in winter,
so savage as a moth
outlive the gudgeon in his humid palaces
the willow is the English olive-tree

           there will be fog in march
in wild grass where it takes an acre to keep a peewit and
    the water soaks your boots and larks rose shivering

           God in the stones
and religion was not a matter of nakedness.

Kapetan Michalis

HE HAS GONE, leaving written papers.
To many houses, all stone and sky,
some green growth in summer, some deep snow in spring.
Thousands of words of dream scribbled on a bedsheet.
This man tore down the fruit from solitude unripe.

In these woods, in the first leaf of the elm
when stone becomes shadow
the most tormented mind is motionable
it will be stony,
can settle among trees like an enormous butterfly
and shadow becomes stone.

Has gone away through the woods.
Where you hear birds now and then.
Small bodies, shrill voices,
a hundred juliets in balconies of branches.
Indoors at night the yellow globe
illuminating nothing.
Words written in the light of death.
It measures time, ripens without falling.
By now has gone a long way through the woods.

He is above the snowline,
in yellow and white clouds swirling marble
coughed out a star a tiny speck of blood.
You cannot know. You only know that he went on.
Am in this poem like a monastery
inscribing words on air and on darkness,
with the texture of rocks and villages
and the sea's unripeness.

Which is neither mine nor his, but in common.

I IMAGINE where God has never been
and a landscape Adam has never seen,
say a broad estuary
crabapple salty on the crooked bough
different from the places we live now;

and I imagine by that estuary
and grape colours and long tones of the sea
quite a new kind of poem
without excuses: thistle, sand and reed
are their own explanation like the creed.

Inland birds cannot enter the poem,
because they carry an intense light with them,
streams of old-fashioned skies;
and half human bird-noises will not fit:
night falls heavy, seabirds understand it.

52

A special edition signed by the author, limited to fifty copies, has been printed on Glastonbury Ivory antique laid and bound in buckram.

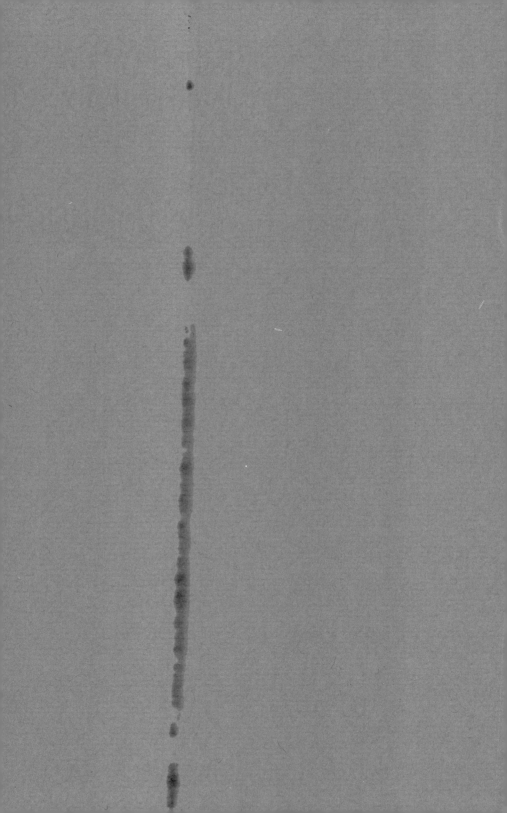